ROYAL JUBILEE

Judith Millidge

SHIRE PUBLICATIONS

Published in Great Britain in 2012 by Shire Publications
Ltd, Midland House, West Way, Botley, Oxford OX2 0PH,
United Kingdom.

44-02 23rd Street, Suite 219, Long Island City, NY 11101,
USA.

E-mail: shire@shirebooks.co.uk   www.shirebooks.co.uk

A CIP catalogue record for this book is available from the
British Library.

Shire Library no. 698.   ISBN-13: 978 0 74781 167 1

Judith Millidge has asserted her right under the Copyright,
Designs and Patents Act, 1988, to be identified as the
author of this book.

Designed by Tony Truscott Designs, Sussex, UK
and typeset in Perpetua and Gill Sans.

Printed in China through Worldprint Ltd.

12 13 14 15 16   10 9 8 7 6 5 4 3 2 1

COVER IMAGE
Queen Victoria's coach draws up outside St Paul's
Cathedral during her Diamond Jubilee celebrations in
1897. Painting by G. S. Amato (fl.1897–1914).

TITLE PAGE IMAGE
The gold state coach in the Mall taking the Queen and the
Duke of Edinburgh to the Service of Thanksgiving at
St Paul's Cathedral to celebrate Elizabeth II's Golden
Jubilee, 2002.

CONTENTS PAGE IMAGE
A commemorative postcard published in 1935, showing
the king's principal residences.

ACKNOWLEDGEMENTS
Bridgeman Art Library/The Royal Collection, pages 24–5;
Bridgeman Art Library/Towneley Hall Art Gallery, cover
and pages 34–5; Guildhall Art Gallery, City of London,
pages 44–5; Library and Archives of Canada/W. and D.
Downey, page 22 (bottom); Library and Archives of
Canada/Mayall & Co., page 32; Library and Archives of
Canada/Topley Studio, page 36; Corbis, pages 10, 54, 55,
and 57; Getty Images, pages 46, 51 (bottom) and 56;
Library of Congress, pages 8, 11, 26 (top), 31 (bottom),
33 (top), and 39 (top); London Gazette, page 22 (top);
Mary Evans Picture Library, pages 14, 17 (top), 20, 39
(middle); Royal Household, pages 59 and 60; Topfoto,
pages 1, 16, and 40; V&A Images, page 19.

Individual contributors: Author's Collection, pages 3, 7
(both), 13 (bottom), 26 (bottom), 27 (bottom), 30, 36
(bottom), 42 (both) 43, 47 (both), 52 (top), 53 (all), 57
(both); Carol Drew, page 61; Norna Exton, pages 26
(middle), 39 (bottom); Barry Freeman Photography, page
48; Terje Hartberg, page 37 (right); Jack Kozik, page 50
(top); Nilo Manalo, page 7 (left); Peter Martens, page 29;
Andy Miller, page 15; Damon Mitchel, page 4; Brian
Mossemenear, page 13 (top); Gillian Moy, page 52
(bottom); George Nicholson, page 18; Mike Peckett, page
36 (top); Puckerings Antiques, page 23; Alice Jaegar
Smith, page 6 (bottom); Randy Robertson, page 6 (top);
John Rochon, page 31 (top); Claire Sutton, page 51 (top);
Marc Teilemann, page 27 (top); Tony Worrall Photography,
page 50 (bottom).

With grateful thanks to all my family and friends who dug
deep into their attics for jubilee memorabilia.

Shire Publications is supporting the Woodland Trust, the UK's leading woodland conservation charity, by funding the dedication of trees.

CONTENTS

INTRODUCTION

M ONARCHIES are a rare breed. In the last century more hereditary rulers lost their crowns than survived long enough to celebrate dozens of years of glorious rule upon the throne; nevertheless, a number of royal jubilees were celebrated around the world, from the diamond jubilee of the venerable Austro-Hungarian Emperor Franz Joseph in 1908, to the sixtieth anniversary of His Majesty King Bhumibol Adulyadej of Thailand in 2006. The British, who pride themselves on the quality of their ceremonial pageantry, have celebrated the jubilees of the kings and queens of Great Britain since 1809, the year of George III's fiftieth anniversary, when the whole country was invited to join in a day of national rejoicing.

Over the last thousand years, fourteen British monarchs have achieved at least twenty-five years on the throne: Ethelred the Unready, Henry I, Henry II, Henry III, Edward I, Edward III, Henry VI, Henry VIII, Elizabeth I, George II, George III, Victoria, George V, and Elizabeth II. Henry III, Edward III and George III survived fifty years, as did James VI and I, as King of Scotland, and of course Victoria and Elizabeth II have reached sixty years on the throne.

The word 'jubilee' is defined by the *Oxford English Dictionary* firstly as 'a special anniversary of an event, especially one celebrating twenty-five or fifty years of a reign or activity', and secondly as 'a period of remission from the penal consequences of sin, granted by the Roman Catholic Church under certain conditions for a year, usually at intervals of twenty-five years'. Secular jubilees owe their origins to sacred jubilees, as described in the Book of Leviticus. The word itself is derived from Hebrew *yobel*, meaning 'ram's horn trumpet', the instrument which was used to proclaim a jubilee year. The idea of a special year of remission of sins and universal pardon was known throughout medieval times, but the first documented religious jubilee was instituted in 1300 by Pope Boniface VIII, who promised the 'broadest forgiveness of sins' to those who visited St Peter's in Rome during that year. This first religious jubilee was immensely popular and the ritual continues today.

Opposite:
Queen Elizabeth II on walkabout in Aylesbury, Buckinghamshire, 2002. The Queen visited seventy cities and towns across Britain between May and August 2002.

Right and below: The Porta Sancta in St Peter's Basilica, Rome, is opened only once every twenty-five years, in a holy jubilee year. The Pope uses the silver hammer to crack open the brick wall and open the door to pilgrims.

Secular jubilees celebrating a monarch's reign are dependent on regnal life spans and are therefore irregular occurrences, but in the nineteenth century in Britain they absorbed the religious traditions of remitting sins and freeing prisoners. Incidentally, it was not until the late nineteenth century that jubilees were accorded the same epithets as wedding anniversaries: silver for twenty-five years, gold for fifty and diamond for sixty.

Henry III was the first English monarch to achieve fifty years on the throne, but his reign was by no means easy or especially peaceful. He inherited the throne at the age of nine in 1216, just a year after his father (King John) had signed the Magna Carta, the first great charter of rights that paved the way for modern democratic government. Henry proved to be a strong and pious king, who was especially devoted to the to the cult of St Edward the Confessor. By 1266, the fiftieth anniversary of his accession, Henry had only just emerged from the bitter struggle of the Second Barons' War, in which he had ultimately triumphed at the battle of Evesham. It was indeed a year of royal celebration, but it was also one in which vicious retribution was carried out on the enemies of the king. The

Dictum of Kenilworth, which was issued almost fifty years to the day from Henry's accession, was a pragmatic document that allowed the surviving rebels to buy back their forfeited lands and confirmed the legitimacy of the Magna Carta, but it also left no one in any doubt that royal authority rested on the king alone.

Just over one hundred years later, in 1377, Edward III achieved the equivalent of his golden jubilee. The founder of the Order of the Garter, and king at a time when the chivalric ideal was at its

PLAYER'S CIGARETTES

EDWARD III

PLAYER'S CIGARETTES

HENRY III

These portraits of Henry III and Edward III, two of Britain's longest-reigning monarchs, are part of a set of cigarette cards, issued by John Player & Son for George V's Silver Jubilee in 1935.

strongest, Edward was in many ways responsible for the origins of the pageantry still associated with great royal occasions. He was the father of nine children, and the concept of a 'royal family' became a strong one. Edward ensured that his five sons were given responsibilities, lands and titles, and as a consequence none ever rebelled against him. His wars with France meant that the noblemen of England were occupied with matters abroad, and so had less time to challenge royal power at home. Despite war and the ravages of the Black Death, in 1377, after forty years of domestic peace, there was much to celebrate, and when Edward died in June of that year (just five months short of the actual anniversary of accession), there were, according to the chronicler Jean Froissart, 'great sorrows made in England', as the king's body was transported through London from the royal palace at Sheen to Westminster in an open coffin.

National celebrations of royal coronations, births, deaths and marriages were difficult in the days before good mass communication – by the end of the eighteenth century news travelled more quickly across Britain thanks to the improvement in road construction, so an event in London could be public knowledge in York, for example, just thirty-six hours later (earlier in the century the same journey would have taken four days). Moreover, increased literacy among the population meant that in the urban centres at any rate, newspapers and pamphlets were read and discussed in coffee houses and their news disseminated to a wide audience.

The first national royal jubilee was celebrated in 1809 and at first glance it seems an unlikely event: George III had suffered bouts of unpopularity,

Well-heeled crowds lean out of their carriages to watch the thanksgiving service held on the steps of St Paul's Cathedral for Queen Victoria's Diamond Jubilee in 1897.

madness and bad luck, losing the American colonies and fathering a brood of dissipated children, only one of whom produced a legitimate heir by the time of the National Jubilee. Subsequent royal jubilees, notably those celebrated in 1935 and 1977, were planned slightly tentatively during periods of economic hardship and national apathy, but just as in 1809, the celebrations and demonstrations of patriotic fervour proved to be highly memorable.

Over the course of two hundred years, the methods of celebrating have a strong thread of tradition running through them: the royal family

Above: Although the people of Chester would have preferred a statue of Queen Victoria to commemorate the 1897 jubilee, enough money was collected for the city to commission this ornate clock, which was unveiled two years later on Queen Victoria's eightieth birthday.

Left: Once part of a fountain, this bust of Queen Victoria was unveiled in front of the city hall in Winnipeg, Manitoba in 1898 to celebrate the queen's Diamond Jubilee. It was moved to a nearby park and re-dedicated in 1967.

attends a service of thanksgiving, and statues, clocks and buildings are erected to commemorate the occasion. Moreover, each generation has added its own novelty to the event and the stories of the parties and celebrations are passed down from one generation to the next. Many of the infinite numbers of souvenirs, if not always treasured, are at least stored in a box to be discovered years later, some of them ending up in antique and charity shops.

Pub.ᵈ Oct.ʳ 25ᵗʰ 1810.

George the-IIIᵣᵈ aged-72-1810.

REIGN'D-50-Years. A ROYAL JUBILEE.

Taken at Windsor by R.Dighton. Spring Gardens.

THE NATIONAL JUBILEE, 1809

THE FIRST ENGLISH KING to enjoy a national celebration devoted to his longevity was George III. His jubilee year began on 25 October 1809, the day on which he entered the fiftieth year of his reign.

That the country celebrated the jubilee of George III at all is surprising. Born two months prematurely on 4 June 1738, the infant Prince George was a tiny child who was baptised immediately because it was considered unlikely that he would survive. In 1788 he suffered such a severe attack of porphyria that it was rumoured he had died, and the attacks of 'madness' (as they were diagnosed) recurred in the early years of the nineteenth century.

George III was the second child and first son of Frederick, Prince of Wales, a man who was detested by his parents, King George II and Queen Caroline. Frederick appears to have been a devoted father, however, and was a generous patron of the arts and sciences (including Thomas Arne, who composed the patriotic *Rule Britannia*). News of Frederick's premature death aged forty-four in 1751 was received with indifference by his father George II, who said rather heartlessly, 'This has been a fatal year to my family. I have lost my eldest son but I was glad of it'.

Young Prince George was created Prince of Wales a month after his father's death and his grandfather took over his education, changing his tutors and ensuring that the prince was raised in seclusion away from the corrupting influence of court and society. When George II died in 1760, Prince George inherited the throne at the age of twenty-two.

George III emerged as a shy, intelligent and considerate man, who became an uxorious husband and father to fifteen children. He was faithful to his wife and interested in the lives of his subjects and the industry of his kingdom. Modest in his habits, he was depicted by the satirists as 'Farmer George'. Though conscientious and pious himself, he somehow failed to pass on these qualities to his sons, all of whom became the butt of derisive jokes because of their extravagant and licentious lifestyles.

In spite of the dubious reputation of some members of the royal family, the ageing king had won the respect and sympathy of his subjects, and public

Opposite:
A rather affectionate portrait painted in honour of George III's jubilee in 1810. The portrait was apparently made from life at Windsor Castle and shows the king in dress uniform wearing the star of the Order of the Garter.

'A new way to pay the national debt', a typically disrespectful cartoon of the royal family by the satirist James Gillray. The king and queen are depicted standing unmercifully in front of the Treasury as the recipients of government funds, their pockets overflowing with coins.

calls for a jubilee celebration began in 1809 with letters to the press. An anonymous correspondent to *The Times*, who signed himself 'Jubal', informed his readers of the biblical precedents relating to jubilees and called on readers to celebrate a national jubilee. A letter from a clergyman on 5 October 1809 urged the archbishops and bishops of Great Britain to ensure that the National Jubilee was celebrated with public acts of worship, 'as far more appropriate to the occasion than the tumult, the riot and excess' proposed by the secular authorities. Other writers thought that instead of spending money on illuminations, the same sum should be devoted to poor relief. One correspondent (the anonymous 'Homo Sum') wrote on 22 September 1809:

> But let us do some real good on this day; let us do something that will never be forgotten either by the king or the People; let us act like sensible Englishmen .... Simply then, let us have no illuminations – an expression of rejoicing common to every state-holiday, common to every country in Europe; but let us rejoice in making others happy.

One of the commemorative medals issued at the time of his jubilee stated that George III was 'beloved by his people, his actions the glory of all his subjects and the veneration of all the world'. Hyperbole aside, the king's reign was a remarkable one, occurring as it did at a time of extreme change – the Industrial Revolution altered living and working conditions, agrarian reforms

In 1810 the Dunston Pillar (a tower over 100 feet tall) in Lincolnshire was topped by a statue of George III in honour of the king's jubilee. It was partially dismantled in 1940 as the tower's height was a danger to low-flying aircraft and is now on display in the grounds of Lincoln Castle.

A commemorative token minted for the 1809 jubilee. The inscription above the king's head reads: '1760 George the III Reigns 1809'. On the reverse there is an imperial crown above a sword and sceptre entwined with ribbon with the inscription, 'National Jubilee of George III'.

impoverished country dwellers, and income tax had been introduced. The discovery of Australia in 1770 by Captain James Cook opened up a whole new area of the world to be explored and exploited by British merchants and adventurers. Britain lost her American colonies in 1781 after a long war, but by the time of the jubilee the country's dominions had actually increased. Although Britain had since 1789 been embroiled in an expensive and debilitating war with France, the Royal Navy was undoubtedly the most powerful in the world and held together the outposts of the country's growing empire alongside Britain's merchant fleet. Britain's maritime forces enabled the nation to live up to Napoleon's jibe that the British were a nation of shopkeepers – in fact, the country's mercantile skills ensured that the nation prospered.

There was a great sense of national pride that Britain actually had a monarch, unlike the French who had lost theirs to the Revolutionaries, and who, by 1809, were ruled by the much-vilified Napoleon Bonaparte. The war with France and the fact that Britain alone held out against the all-conquering French was a source of immense patriotism, which was focused on the king himself. The British (or at least the chattering classes) were very conscious of the fact that, unlike the rest of Europe, they were free of 'the yoke of foreign tyranny' (in the words of the author of *An Account of the Celebration of the Jubilee*) and in 1809 they were determined to celebrate this.

Furthermore, the monarchy as an institution was secure and the line of succession was clear, through the Prince of Wales and then to his daughter Princess Charlotte, the king's sole legitimate grandchild. Indeed, the British royal family had seldom been quite so numerous: the surviving children of King George and Queen Charlotte numbered seven princes and six

George III and Queen Charlotte had fifteen children, thirteen of whom survived infancy. Brought up strictly, their sons rebelled by living lives of dissolution, while their daughters were kept in seclusion at Windsor.

princesses of the royal blood in 1809. The lifestyles of the king's children were the subject of bawdy debate in the pamphlets and papers of the day and they were certainly not held in universal respect. Nevertheless, at the time of the National Jubilee they received the deference accorded to their rank.

The king and queen were reasonably popular and admired for their virtuous and modest lifestyles. The king's increasing infirmity (aged seventy-two, he was almost blinded by cataracts) also attracted a great deal of sympathy. Moreover, they were accessible and were often seen at Windsor, Kew and in London. Although the king and queen travelled little around the kingdom, the king had become fond of Weymouth, which he had first visited in 1789 to convalesce from his attack of porphyria. On subsequent visits, he was cheered on his journey and people flocked to see the royal family stroll along the beach. The town of Weymouth was forever thankful to its royal visitors, because they made the town fashionable and popular. In the year of the king's jubilee the citizens erected a wonderful statue of the king, inscribed simply:

George III was extremely fond of the seaside resort of Weymouth, which he visited regularly from 1789, and the townspeople returned his affection. This statue was erected as a tribute to the town's royal patron in 1810.

The grateful inhabitants
To George the Third
On entering the 50th year of his reign.

THE NATIONAL JUBILEE CELEBRATIONS, 1809

A month before the great day, the Common Council of the City of London resolved to celebrate the king's jubilee with a procession, a service of thanksgiving, and, after some deliberation, a dinner. *The Times* reported on 16 September: '[the Council has] resolved unanimously that this court will celebrate the approaching anniversary of His Majesty's accession to the throne of this kingdom on the 25th day of October next, being the day on which His Majesty will enter the fiftieth year of his reign'.

The City's decision and the Lord Mayor's example were echoed around the country, as towns and villages organised communal celebrations that were largely funded by wealthy local landowners. The festivities consisted mainly of eating, drinking, illuminations and fireworks, and included people of every rank. Towns and cities up and down the country held ox roasts or beef teas, and dispensed plum pudding or strong liquor to the poor. Religious services of thanksgiving

A view of the celebrations that took place outside the Mansion House, London, on 25 October 1809, to mark the Golden Jubilee of King George III.

were held in churches of all denominations. Local volunteer militia paraded, fifty-gun salutes were fired, and loyal toasts were drunk over and over again.

On 25 October, the biggest procession in London was undertaken by the Lord Mayor in his spectacular golden coach (which only slightly pre-dated the king's reign), before a service of thanksgiving and a splendid dinner (including 'a plentiful supply of Madeira') in the Egyptian Hall of the Mansion House.

The lords of the Admiralty decreed that all serving sailors should be entertained with roast beef and plum pudding, washed down by a pint of wine or half a pint of rum 'in addition to their usual allowance'.

The king granted a free pardon to all military deserters and to all debtors who owed money to the Crown. Prisoners of war were released, with the exception of the French, owing to 'the unparalleled severity of their ruler in detaining all British subjects in France'.

In Birmingham a magnificent statue of the 'ever to be lamented hero', Viscount Nelson, was unveiled at midnight on 24 October, a few days after the official anniversary of the Battle of Trafalgar. This was a highlight of Birmingham's jubilee celebrations, and despite the lateness of the hour attracted a crowd of five thousand spectators who broke down the protective scaffolding around the monument in their eagerness to see it.

The royal family remained at Windsor for the day and attended a private service of thanksgiving in St George's Chapel. After the service the king inspected the militia and artillery, which were assembled to fire the salute, but he did not take part in any further public celebrations. By all accounts, however, the rest of the family made up for his absence. Queen Charlotte, accompanied

In the biblical spirit of jubilees, this Victorian illustration shows three-penny bits being distributed to French prisoners of war at Portsmouth in 1809.

GRAND NATIONAL JUBILEE
celebrated
OCTOBER 25ᵀᴴ 1809.
THE BACHELORS OF WINDSOR
hereby gratefully record the condescension of
HER MAJESTY QUEEN CHARLOTTE
and her AUGUST FAMILY
in honouring them with their presence
in this ACRE
to witness the roasting of an OX.
the gift of R.O. FENWICK. ESQ.,
of the ROYAL HORSE GUARDS BLUE.
of which as also Plum Puddings
provided by the BACHELORS.
they graciously partook
amidst the acclamations of the joyful populace
to whom this OLD ENGLISH FARE
was distributed.

This plaque in Bachelors Acre, Windsor, marks the spot where Queen Charlotte and members of the royal family attended an ox roast to celebrate the jubilee. The king, who was almost blind, was deemed too frail to join in the festivities.

by a number of her children, attended an ox roast that was organised in Bachelors Acre in Windsor, and then went on to host a 'fête' at Frogmore. The fête encompassed a series of extravagant patriotic displays: there were three flights of rockets, a display of balloons ascending above the party, and on the lake, Britannia was pulled to and fro in chariots drawn by 'sea-horses'. This was followed by 'an elegant supper consisting of all the delicacies of the season'. Inhabitants of Windsor who had made donations to be distributed among the poor were invited to Frogmore, where there were 'a great number of tradesmen's wives and daughters present, mixed with the first nobility'. It is safe to say that a good time was had by all, as the jollifications continued until 4 a.m.

In January 1810, the radical MP Sir Francis Burdett referred to the jubilee as 'a clumsy trick, to thrust joy down the throats of people'. Contemporary accounts, however, suggest that people were quite happy to join in with the national rejoicing. While the memories of the celebration of the National Jubilee no doubt lingered long in the minds of those who took part, the residents of Nuneham Courtenay, a small village in Oxfordshire, made a far-reaching decision that affected the lives of all the children born in 1810. Each baby was to be christened Jubilee George or Jubilee Charlotte, which was a permanent reminder of the event. Twelve children were born in 1810 – eight Georges and four Charlottes.

It is fortunate that the country chose to celebrate George III's jubilee at the beginning of his fiftieth year on the throne, because by the time of the precise anniversary he was even more frail. Celebrations in October 1810 were muted because of the illness of the king's youngest daughter, Princess Amelia, who was dying of tuberculosis. On 26 October 1810 *The Times* reported:

Most of the streets of the West End of the Town were illuminated last night.
It was generally understood that such demonstrations of joy would not be agreeable to the royal family on account of the alarming state of the Princess Amelia, and, therefore, no preparations were made for the occasion.

After the princess's death in November that year, George III's mental health declined irreparably and he spent the remaining ten years of his reign confined to Windsor Castle, often unaware of who he was, let alone his status as Britain's longest-lived monarch.

The Jubilee, by John Harris. This colourful board game has 150 spaces, each one detailing an event of George III's reign, from his accession in 1760 to his jubilee in 1809. The publisher hoped that the events recorded would 'create a lively interest in the breast of every juvenile Briton'.

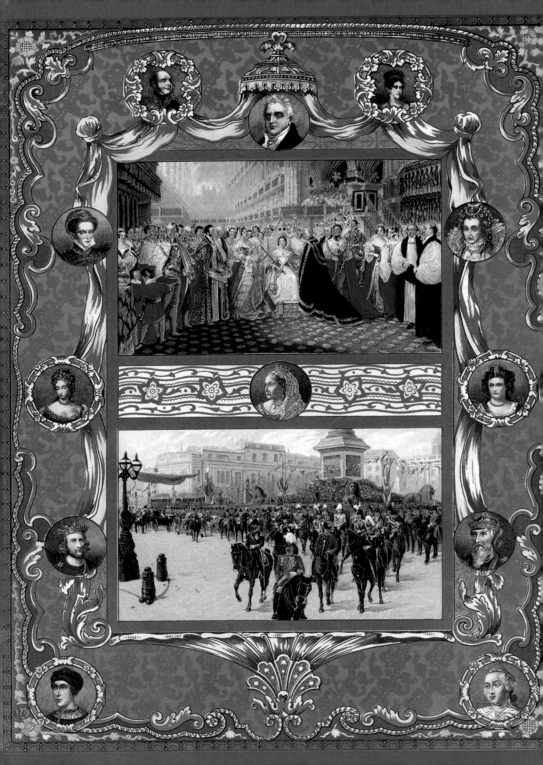

QUEEN VICTORIA'S JUBILEES

QUEEN VICTORIA acceded to the throne on 20 June 1837, on the death of her uncle, King William IV. The daughter of Edward, Duke of Kent, the fourth son of George III, she was one of only six legitimate grandchildren of George III, although she had more than a dozen illegitimate cousins. Victoria had been brought up in seclusion by her mother after her father's death in 1820, and, aged eighteen at the time of William IV's death, she was more than ready to cast off the shackles of maternal restriction. Three years later she married her cousin Prince Albert of Saxe-Coburg-Gotha, and their famously happy marriage produced a dynasty. When Albert died prematurely in 1861, Victoria was prostrate with grief and largely retreated from public view for many years. There was no question of her celebrating the Silver Jubilee of her reign in 1862.

By the time of her Golden Jubilee, over a quarter of a century had elapsed since Victoria began her self-imposed exile from public life and the queen's popularity had dipped alarmingly during that time. When public murmurings began to advocate a jubilee celebration, the queen's very longevity and her position at the head of a great nation and large family restored her public prestige.

THE GOLDEN JUBILEE, 1887

In 1886, when she entered the fiftieth year of her reign, there were several congratulatory articles in the newspapers, which the queen read with pleasure. Victoria began to revel in the acclaim of the people, while modestly denying that personal popularity was something that she sought. 'I don't want or like flattery, but I am very thankful and encouraged by these marks of affection and appreciation of my efforts', she wrote in her journal.

The first public suggestion that the Golden Jubilee should be celebrated came, once again, from the press with a letter in *The Times*. Gladstone's Liberal government was not keen to be involved, partly for reasons of cost, and even when the Conservatives took over under Lord Salisbury in the summer of 1886, politicians were reluctant to use public funds. So the

Opposite:
The Illustrated London News published a special jubilee issue, which included colour illustrations of scenes from the queen's life.

occasion was funded by the Crown, and the queen was able to dictate exactly how she would celebrate the occasion. Westminster Abbey was chosen as the venue for a service of thanksgiving that would be attended by the extensive royal family, politicians, foreign dignitaries and less exalted members of the public, including ninety journalists. The queen took the trouble to ensure that the religious service was relatively short, requesting that 'there should be no discourse or sermon: because at that time of year the weather is likely to be hot; and in hot weather her strength fails her almost entirely'.

Queen Victoria was delighted by the 'more than kind reception' she received during her Golden Jubilee celebrations. She conveyed her formal thanks to the nation via the pages of *The London Gazette*.

A portrait of Queen Victoria issued for her Golden Jubilee. The queen wears the small diamond crown created especially for her in 1870, which was designed to be worn over her widow's veil.

The press was responsible for encouraging the rest of the nation to celebrate the great day, and official and commercial institutions marked the anniversary by erecting permanent memorials or by appending the royal coat of arms or visage to their products. Crockery, commemorative medals, badges and textiles were mass-produced and eagerly snapped up by the public. In January 1887 the Prince of Wales, knowing that his mother would dislike the suggestion that she take a significant public role in her forthcoming jubilee celebrations, softened her up by presenting her with a tasteful souvenir in the form of a jubilee inkstand. The queen pronounced it 'very pretty and useful' and continued to take an active interest in preparations thereafter. In the year leading up to her Golden Jubilee, Queen Victoria pleaded age and infirmity in order to escape from an exceptionally busy programme of events. She was, after all, sixty-eight and suffering from the minor infirmities that age brings, and she felt that the Prince of Wales could bear the brunt of the work.

As the anniversary drew nearer, the queen became more involved in the preparations. She signed innumerable pardons for prisoners across the Empire – although she declined to forgive one criminal for his cruelty to animals.

Queen Victoria was overwhelmed, delighted and exhausted by the three days of festivities and recorded them meticulously in her journal. On 20 June 1887, she travelled from Windsor Castle to Buckingham Palace for a 'large family dinner'. Numerous members of her extended family had travelled across Europe for the jubilee and the royal apartments were overflowing. Members of the nobility, such as Earl Spencer, volunteered to put up some of the royal visitors in their London houses, although the queen's eldest daughter, the Crown Princess of Prussia, had to stay in an hotel in south London.

On 21 June, 'the royalties' lined up for the procession and service of thanksgiving in Westminster Abbey. It was a magnificent sight, with the princes clad in superb uniforms, the massed bands of the British army, and a contingent of the Indian army adding even more colour. Empress of India since 1876, Victoria was also queen of South Africa, Canada, Australia and New Zealand, as well as numerous smaller colonies. Approximately one-quarter of the world's population owed allegiance to the Queen-Empress: she truly was the ruler of an empire on which the sun never set and her loyal subjects arrived in their thousands to celebrate her Golden Jubilee. The procession to Westminster Abbey was enlivened by the exotic presence of several magnificently attired Indian princes, as well as the queen and crown princess of Hawaii, and princes from Persia, Japan and Siam among the European dignitaries. Victoria herself stubbornly refused to wear state robes or a crown, despite the pleas of her family. She stood out as a small, black-clad figure in a sea of colourful uniforms and gorgeous silks during the

The crown on this charming brass inkstand is hinged, and lifts off to expose the inkwell. The Prince of Wales presented a similar inkstand to his mother in 1887 at the beginning of her jubilee year.

magnificent processions, her only concession being a bonnet and veil lavishly trimmed with white lace and diamonds.

Surrounded by her family and basking in the respect and reverence of millions, the queen recorded rather poignantly, 'I sat alone (oh! without my beloved husband, for whom this would have been such a proud day!)'

PUBLIC CELEBRATIONS AT HOME

Church services were held across Britain, and many towns celebrated with garden parties, municipal dinners, processions and fireworks. Children were entertained everywhere, from the grand tea and entertainment in Hyde Park attended by thirty thousand East End children and the queen herself, to the

The Family of Queen Victoria was painted at Windsor by Laurits Regner Tuxen in 1887. He shows the queen surrounded by her surviving children, their spouses and some of her forty grandchildren.

smaller but no less enthusiastic parties elsewhere. In Preston there was a procession of sixteen thousand Church of England schoolchildren, and in Portsmouth the wives and children of the soldiers in the garrison were invited to a garden party in Government House, where they enjoyed an ample tea and music played by the band of the Worcestershire Regiment. On the night of 21 June, bonfires were lit across Britain and several correspondents to *The Times* reported on the number of fires visible from high points across the nation.

Left: Engraved with a rose, shamrock and thistle as symbols of the British nations, surmounted by a horseshoe for good luck, and topped by a royal crown, this silver brooch was converted into a necklace and was manufactured in Birmingham in 1886.

A hand-tinted photograph of the Jubilee Clock erected on the promenade in Weymouth to celebrate Queen Victoria's Golden Jubilee.

Below: Pressed glass was used to mass-produce cheap but wonderfully decorative commemorative items for the jubilee. Many companies used the same patterns ten years later in 1897.

The jubilee souvenir industry began in earnest in 1887. Cups, mugs, plates, badges and jewellery were available for sale and are still collectable today. This china cup and saucer is decorated with the royal arms and has gilt edging.

The Golden Jubilee provided an opportunity to review the progress of the nation since 1837. Scientific, industrial, social and democratic changes had transformed Britain, and the Queen's subjects were, by and large, duly grateful and proud. *The Times* devoted several thousand words to an exhaustive review of the nation's progress and position in the wider world, ending with the sober reflection that, 'while the British Empire has thus been growing at home and abroad other States have by no means been stationary'.

CELEBRATIONS THROUGHOUT THE EMPIRE

Just as in 1809, local celebrations took place all over Great Britain, but in 1887 the main difference was that the rest of the world joined in. A statue was erected in Singapore, 'by the Chinese community … to be placed in the Government House as a memorial of the loyal affection of Her Majesty's

This plate is a visual summary of the imperial achievements of the queen's reign. The iconography of the empire demonstrates great pride in the queen and 'the empire on which the sun never sets'.

In 1887 a new design was issued for gold and silver coins, depicting a more mature Queen Victoria, wearing her small coronet. This is an 1887 jubilee sovereign, which shows St George and the dragon on the reverse.

Chinese subjects and of their gratitude for the benefit of her rule.' The jubilee itself extended to the poorest members of society and the lepers of Singapore were no doubt grateful to receive an extra dole of rice as part of the city's festivities.

From Yokohama to York, and Cardiff to Cape Town, the queen's jubilee was 'heartily celebrated', with fireworks, dinners, church services and illuminations. In India it was the monsoon season, the time of the year when the officers of the Raj retreated to the cool of the Indian hill stations. Nevertheless, although the season was 'unfavourable for public ceremonies', as *The Times* reported, the day did not pass by unnoticed. Jubilee day was a public holiday and fifty-gun salutes were fired in the major cities and garrisons of the subcontinent. The Governor of Madras unveiled a statue of the queen in Calcutta and the entire city was illuminated, while in the cooler climes of Simla, there was a grand ball. Certain categories of military prisoners were granted an amnesty, and some were released entirely.

Many institutions took the opportunity to construct lasting memorials that were to prove useful to succeeding generations. Drinking troughs and water fountains, libraries and hospitals were built around the empire. In Mysore the Maharajah laid the foundation stone for the Victoria Jubilee Institute, and the Queen Victoria Jubilee Burial and Burning Ground was opened at Mithi in Sind – possibly the most unusual jubilee memorial of them all. In South Africa, the foundation stone was laid for the new legislative building in Pietermaritzburg in Natal. Similarly, in Canada the inhabitants of Stratford in Perth County, Ontario, opened their new courthouse with a jubilee party costing $500. Statues of the queen proliferated, one of the finest going up on the queen's doorstep just outside the gates at Windsor Castle.

Details of the events in London were telegraphed around the world and reported breathlessly to the queen's subjects across the globe. The New Zealand *Daily Telegraph* noted that the scenes in London were 'unparalleled for brilliancy and wealth of colour', but also reported that 'heavy winds and drizzling rain prevented effective illuminations' in Dunedin, New Zealand. It is unclear whether it was the depressing weather or the excitement of the occasion that drove two women to exceed 'the bounds of temperance': the paper reported that they appeared before magistrates on a charge of being drunk and disorderly, but were 'treated leniently on account of the Queen's Jubilee'.

THE DIAMOND JUBILEE, 1897

Queen Victoria's Golden Jubilee was called 'the most splendid spectacle of the century', and few thought there would be another great royal jubilee in their lifetime. The nation reckoned without the stamina and longevity of Queen Victoria, however, who was in remarkably good health ten years later,

Opposite:
The Jubilee Monument was erected in Calcutta, the capital city of British India, for Queen Victoria's Diamond Jubilee. The monumental statue, which is two-and-a-half times life size, was sculpted by Sir George Frampton and cast in light bronze.

despite the burdens of office, personal worries and the infirmities of age. Mindful of her own mortality, the queen announced that no celebrations should take place until she had actually reached the anniversary of her sixtieth year on the throne. On 26 September 1896 she wrote:

> Today is the day on which I have reigned longer, by a day, than any English sovereign, and the people wished to make all sorts of demonstrations, which I asked them not to do until I had completed sixty years next June.

She made it clear that she was 'not personally desirous of any festivities', but she recognised that the nation and the empire wanted to express their loyalty and gratitude. She remembered how she had been exhausted by several days of state dinners and functions in 1887 and requested that the celebrations be

Holloway's Souvenir prominently includes the achievements of the entrepreneur, Thomas Holloway, among the events of the queen's reign. Holloway made his fortune peddling mostly harmless pills and potions, and used his fortune to found Royal Holloway College and the Holloway Sanatorium in Surrey.

limited to just one day, 22 June 1897. More importantly, this time, the government would foot the bill. The Golden Jubilee had been a monumental success on every level and in 1897 Lord Salisbury's government could see that another patriotic celebration would do them no harm.

In the months leading up to the festivities, there was some debate about what it should be called. The Home Secretary reminded his colleagues about the biblical origin of jubilees, and suggested terms such as 'Jubilissimee', but it seems to have been the queen herself who intervened and approved the popular terminology recently applied to sixtieth wedding anniversaries. Britain and the empire would celebrate her Diamond Jubilee.

A gaggle of royals arrived from across Europe as in 1887. The queen's eldest grandson, Kaiser Wilhelm of Germany, was unpopular and had offended his grandmother with his interference in a dispute between Turkey and Greece, and was excluded from the guest list. Once again, the royal apartments were overflowing, and the royal family seemingly overcome with excitement. The Empress Frederick (Vicky, the queen's eldest child) wrote: 'Buckingham Palace is like a beehive, & the place is so crammed we do not see so very much of one another'.

On 22 June the queen set out on a six-mile procession through the streets of London in brilliant sunshine. As she left Buckingham Palace, she paused outside the gates to press a button that sent a telegraphic Jubilee Message of thanks around the empire. 'From my heart I thank my beloved people. May

By 1897 the succession to the throne was secured to three generations. This commemorative coin depicts Queen Victoria, her eldest son Albert Edward, Prince of Wales (later Edward VII), her grandson Prince George, Duke of York (later George V) and her great-grandson Prince Edward (later Edward VIII).

Her Majesty Queen Victoria arrives in London from Windsor accompanied by her Highland servants and a small procession of Lifeguards, prior to the official celebrations, which began on 22 June 1897.

The royal procession passing the National Gallery en route to St Paul's Cathedral. The Princess of Wales accompanied Victoria, occasionally patting her hand in comfort when she appeared overwhelmed.

God bless them!' The Commander-in-Chief of the Army, Viscount Wolseley, led the procession, which progressed into the City, pausing outside St Paul's cathedral for a brief thanksgiving service. The queen was too lame to climb the steps to the cathedral, so the service was held outside; fortunately the glorious 'Queen's Weather' lasted for the duration of the service. Her cousin, the Grand Duchess of Mecklenburg-Strelitz, was horrified when she learnt of the plans for the thanksgiving service: '... after sixty years' Reign to thank God in the street!!!' However, the assembled clergy, the troops from around the Empire and the other dignitaries formed a 'most impressive' scene and after the service, the procession continued across London Bridge. Never before had a royal procession driven south of the river, through the

working-class suburbs of Southwark, Bermondsey and Kennington.

For weeks, the personal columns of the newspapers had been taken up with advertisements for rooms along the route, ranging in prices from an expensive 150 guineas for a large room opposite the law courts in Fleet Street and promising 'good lavatory accommodation', to 'no reasonable offer refused' above a shop on the less-desirable Borough High Street.

The sense of pride in London, the capital city at the heart of the empire, was as irresistible as the outpouring of genuine affection for the old lady at the heart of the celebration. The city had spent £250,000 on street decorations and illuminations, and the queen had repeatedly asked the Home Office to ensure that the small houses and stands along the route were not overloaded with spectators. The planners and the queen were rewarded with an unprecedented outpouring of loyalty and patriotism on what the queen called a 'never-to-be-forgotten day'. She wrote in her journal on 22 June:

'Her Majesty's gracious smile', a rare photograph of Queen Victoria smiling, proving that she was most definitely amused by her Diamond Jubilee festivities.

> No one ever, I believe, has met with such an ovation as was given to me, passing through those six miles of streets .... The crowds were quite indescribable and their enthusiasm truly marvelous and deeply touching.

In the event, the celebrations lasted a fortnight, with a garden party at Buckingham Palace on 28 June, a review of Indian and colonial troops in Windsor Great Park on 2 July, a reception of colonial prime ministers on 7 July and a garden party for MPs and their wives at Windsor on 3 July.

The Prince of Wales represented the queen at the great review of the fleet at Spithead on 26 June, which was a very practical demonstration of Britain's imperial might. More than 160 ships were drawn up in four lines stretching along the Solent. *The Times* reported:

> [It] is certainly the most formidable in all its elements and qualities that has ever been brought together, and such as no combination of other nations can rival. It is at once the most powerful and far-reaching weapon which the world has ever seen.

It became a matter of civic pride for towns and cities to celebrate the jubilee in an appropriate manner. At the very least, shops and public buildings were decorated and illuminated at night, but most towns and many villages

Overleaf: *Queen Victoria's Diamond Jubilee Service outside St Paul's Cathedral, 22 June 1897* (oil on canvas) by Gennaro d'Amato. This wonderful image conveys an excellent impression of the scale of the celebrations in 1897. The queen is a tiny purple and black figure amid a sea of scarlet and gold.

Mass-produced tiles and plaques were manufactured in 1897 for use on vernacular buildings. This fine example is on the Old Post Office on the Abingdon Road, Oxford.

The official commemorative medallion for the Diamond Jubilee was produced in gold, silver and bronze versions. The obverse depicts the 'old' head of the queen, used on coins from 1893, while the reverse shows the young Victoria and an inscription which translates as, 'Length of days in her right hand; and glory in her left hand'.

had a parade and a party. There had been disagreement in Birmingham about the nature of the celebrations, because initially the frugal yet philanthropic municipal authorities insisted on endowing hospitals and facilities for the poor and needy, rather than spending money on more frivolous festivities. But popular opinion was strongly in favour of more traditional celebrations, and residents were rewarded with a two-mile procession of the militia, fire brigades, athletic clubs, trade institutions and nine musical bands.

In Manchester forty thousand children were presented with jubilee medals and eleven thousand children from the ragged and industrial schools marched in procession, before receiving a treat and their medal. Gateshead held a similar function, with each child

receiving a paper bag containing two buns and an orange, before being presented with a jubilee medal. At Windsor, there was a festive and floral display, as well as a Venetian fête along the River Thames, which ended with fireworks and illuminations.

In Liverpool buildings were decorated and five of the city's parks hosted amusements and sports for children, concluding with a firework display. The Lord Mayor hosted a garden party and lunch, and there was a spectacular display of mercantile shipping, which extended for five miles. Ships of the Cunard and White Star companies took poor children for cruises around the bay, and in the evening each vessel fired night signals in turn. Many towns, such as Portsmouth and Southend, decorated 'jubilee arches' with flowers, and others erected permanent reminders of the anniversary by building clock towers or statues.

Similar celebrations took place throughout the Empire. In Victoria, British Columbia, visitors flocked into town, 'every man, woman and child wearing medals or badges bearing the well-known features of her whom all the world is now honouring'. In Shanghai the decorations of the British community extended into the French sector, and ex-patriots celebrated with a grand gymkhana and the foundation of the Victoria Nursing Home as a permanent memorial. In India, the Maharajah of Gwalior pardoned and released 10 per cent of his prisoners and laid the foundation stone for a new waterworks.

The emphasis was on ensuring that children and the less fortunate had a day to remember. It worked: as a teenager in 1978 I gave my great-grandmother

Above left: An ornate pinchbeck and enamel brooch, with the queen's portrait decorated with thistles, roses and shamrocks. This is one of hundreds of designs mass-produced to celebrate the Diamond Jubilee.

Above right: Many towns chose to celebrate the jubilee by raising money for charitable or utilitarian purposes. Even a humble water fountain, such as this one in Woolhampton, Berkshire, could encapsulate a nation's pride in its queen.

Cities around the Empire rose to the occasion with decorations and celebrations as heartfelt as those in Britain. Ontario put on a particularly fine display; here is the Canada Atlantic Railway office in Ottawa.

a card for her ninety-sixth birthday, which showed a Victorian street scene during the Diamond Jubilee celebrations. To me, it was an image from ancient history, and when she said, 'of course, my dear, I was there – Father took us up to London for the day', my jaw dropped.

The commemoration of Queen Victoria's sixty-year reign lived on in the memories of those who witnessed it because it combined a genuine gratitude for the stability her reign had provided with a sense of patriotism and pride in Britain's position as the most powerful and influential nation on earth.

Temporary ornamental arches, like the Armorial Arch in Portsmouth, were a prominent feature of patriotic urban decorations in June 1897. Made of wood, plaster or even cardboard, they were covered with flowers, bunting and loyal messages, and went up in towns and cities across Britain and the Empire.

Below: Parties and celebrations were held all over the empire, such as this 'loyal jubilee gathering' in front of the Queen's Statue in Bombay.

AT QUEENS STATUE, BOMBAY

Once again, the designers in the Potteries produced some charming crockery souvenirs for the jubilee. This mug, with its floral and heraldic decoration, is typical.

39

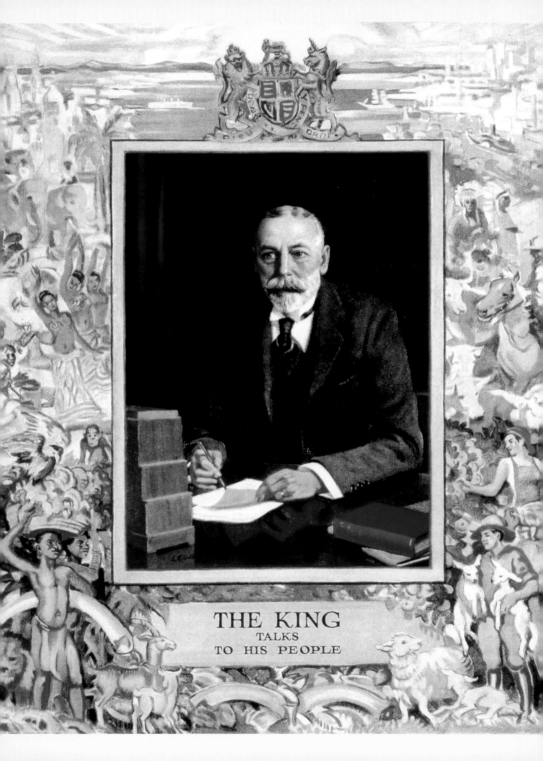

THE KING
TALKS
TO HIS PEOPLE

THE SILVER JUBILEE OF GEORGE V, 1935

WHEN GEORGE V acceded to the throne in 1910, Britain was at the height of her imperial powers, although the king himself was a diffident and shy man who had lived somewhat in the shadow of his charismatic father and long-lived grandmother. The second son of Edward VII, he inherited his place in direct line of succession after the death of his wayward elder brother Prince Albert Victor in 1892. He also inherited his fiancée, Princess May of Teck. When they came to the throne in 1910, King George and Queen Mary had been married for seventeen happy years and shared strongly held values of faith, duty and traditionalism.

The year after his succession George V travelled to India for the magnificent Coronation Durbar in Delhi, in which he and Queen Mary received the homage of the Indian princes. It was a magnificent imperial spectacle and the first and last time that the king-emperor honoured his Indian subjects in such a way. Twenty-five years later, Britain emerged scarred and financially broken from the dreadful slaughter of the First World War, while the imperial peace of India was threatened by the increasingly violent calls for independence. In a quarter of a century, the world had changed radically.

Aside from the effects of the First World War, British society was becoming more fluid by the 1930s: wider educational opportunities, the introduction of social security in the form of unemployment benefit and pensions, and the march of technology and invention meant that power was shifting from the aristocracy to the educated and newly eloquent middle classes. Abroad, despite the well-intentioned edicts of the League of Nations, Germany and Italy were stealthily re-arming and the horrific spectre of another European war hovered on the horizon. Two of King George's first cousins, Kaiser Wilhelm II of Germany and Tsar Nicholas II of Russia, had lost their thrones as a result of the Great War, but the British king-emperor had demonstrated ruthless survival tactics, changing the family surname to Windsor and emerging as a dependable, unchanging figurehead.

The idea of celebrating George V's Silver Jubilee was first mooted in 1934, but the king initially wondered what people would think about the expense,

Opposite:
The Tatler's jubilee issue, 8 May 1936, shows George V broadcasting to the Empire.

King George and
Queen Mary on
their way to the
Service of
Thanksgiving at
St Paul's Cathedral.

Below: 'The
greatest number
of people in the
streets that I have
ever seen in my
life', according to
the king. London
was packed with
visitors eager to
share in the jubilee
celebrations and
to demonstrate
their loyalty
to their king
and queen.

given the very difficult economic circumstances of the time. Britain, and indeed the rest of the Western world, was barely emerging from the Great Depression and unemployment remained a significant problem. 'All this fuss and expense about our Jubilee. What will the people think of it, in these hard and anxious times?' he asked. His ministers believed that a celebration of the king's reign, with all the pageantry and pomp that it would entail, would do the government no harm and would provide a show of unity and might to the rest of the world.

By this time, George V was seventy and felt every one of his years. He had recovered from a life-threatening attack of pneumonia in 1928 and many of his diary entries in the 1930s hint at the fatigue of age. Nevertheless, he and the queen started a busy programme of celebrations in May 1935, beginning with the official Service of Thanksgiving in St Paul's Cathedral on Monday 6 May.

Any qualms that the king had about the popularity of a jubilee celebration must have disappeared as soon as his carriage left the gates of Buckingham Palace. All the way to St Paul's Cathedral, the streets were filled with cheering crowds, many of whom had slept on the streets to be sure of a good view of the elaborate procession. The BBC broadcast the service live and provided a

commentary on the procession, so that for the first time listeners across the globe could share in events as they happened.

The king recorded the details carefully in his journal:

> A never to be forgotten day when we celebrated our Silver Jubilee. It was a glorious summer's day: 75 degrees in the shade. The greatest number of people in the streets that I have ever seen in my life. The enthusiasm was indeed most touching.

An atmospheric view of the interior of St Paul's Cathedral as members of the royal party process down the aisle at the end of the service on 6 May 1935.

The king sent his official thanks to the Dean of St Paul's by telegram, although he expressed rather more trenchant views as he left the cathedral. 'A wonderful service. The Queen and I are most grateful. Just one thing wrong with it – too many damn parsons getting in the way. I didn't know there were so many damn parsons in England.'

The party in London continued well into the night, as crowds danced and sang in the streets and cheered the royal family as they appeared on the balcony of Buckingham Palace. At 10 o'clock the king pressed an electric switch that ignited a fire in Hyde Park, the first in a chain of beacons that were lit across the British Isles to be tended by the Boy Scouts.

Later in the week, the king received a loyal address from both houses of Parliament and, in response to nightly cries of 'We want the king', waved to the crowds from the balcony of Buckingham Palace every night until the weekend. The king and queen continued to mark the event during May with a series of carriage rides through many London boroughs and the Docks. On 26 May,

The Reception of King George V and Queen Mary at St Paul's Cathedral, 1935, by Frank O. Salisbury. Amid the red and gold of the uniforms and regalia, the light falls on the stately figure of Queen Mary beside her husband.

Queen Mary's birthday, they drove through north London accompanied by their grandchildren, princesses Elizabeth and Margaret. Everywhere they were met with flags and bunting and cheering crowds. Several banners in the East End proudly proclaimed, 'Lousy but Loyal', a frank message that would not have been considered proper during the Victorian jubilees.

Despite the king's early misgivings, the nation made extensive preparations for the jubilee festivities on 6 May. The day was declared a public holiday throughout the United Kingdom and town councils and volunteer committees made plans for processions, teas, fêtes, pageants and sports events. In London the Office of Works ensured that major buildings such as the Palace of Westminster, St Paul's Cathedral and Buckingham Palace were floodlit at night and adorned with flowers by day. The Royal Navy prepared to assemble at Spithead for a fleet review, the first since 1924. Manufacturers and advertisers shamelessly applied the word 'jubilee' to all manner of products in an effort to boost sales, from the new K6 'Jubilee' telephone box designed by Sir Giles

Gilbert Scott, to the Jubilee class of steam locomotive employed by the London Midland and Scottish railway. Children were encouraged to take part in historical pageants or march with the boy scouts and girl guides. In Melbourne, Australia, children received special lessons about the monarchy and many acted out the coronation and other scenes from the king's life.

Throughout May, Buckingham Palace was inundated with letters and telegrams of good wishes from ordinary people around the world: the king noted in his journal that 610 arrived in the first post on 6 May, and many thousands followed. Fellow heads of state sent their own messages, including Adolf Hitler, who added (without any apparent irony) that the German people followed 'with warm sympathy all the efforts of Your Majesty and the British Government for the consolidation of peace.'

The basic format of the 1935 jubilee was not so very different from the events of 1897, although the organisation perhaps lacked the inherent paternalism of the Victorian arrangements. The levelling effect of the Great War and the Depression meant that those in positions of power did not simply assume that 'the people' would automatically respond with displays of patriotism. While the official events of Victoria's jubilees had been concentrated in London, in 1935 the government ensured that the provinces were included. The king's sons were despatched to Scotland, Northern Ireland and Wales to represent their father at ceremonies on Saturday 11 May.

The Prince of Wales was cheered by a crowd of 100,000 in Cardiff, where he spent the day laying a wreath at the Welsh National War Memorial, lunching

Residents of Dudley Street, Paddington, London, at the start of their jubilee festivities in honour of King George V. Street parties were especially popular in the poorer districts of the cities.

with 'representatives of Welsh life' in the City Hall, and attending a children's party at Cardiff Arms Park, the city's great rugby stadium. At the same time his younger brother, the Duke of York, was attending festivities in Edinburgh with his wife, while the Duke of Gloucester was awarded the freedom of Belfast during his visit to Northern Ireland.

Across the Empire, people celebrated enthusiastically. In India, where the Congress Party led vociferous demands for Indian independence, a distinction was made between the person of the king-emperor and the imperial government. The official celebrations across the subcontinent therefore went ahead without trouble as people were keen to show their respect and affection for King George and Queen Mary. Public buildings were illuminated for a week, the king's broadcast was relayed to large crowds, and thousands travelled to see fireworks and Bengali dancing in Calcutta. The viceroy attended a Jubilee Tattoo in Simla, which featured an extraordinary mix of ancient and modern military skills, and culminated in a firework display with the letters GR and a large crown blazing against the Himalayan foothills.

Hong Kong celebrated with snaking processions of silver-scaled dragons, which were regarded as symbols of good fortune. *The Times* reported that each of the 1,800 scales was inscribed with 'The King's Jubilee' and although about one hundred were snatched, the remainder were distributed to local officials as mementoes of the occasion.

Since 1932, the king had spoken to the nation each Christmas by delivering a broadcast from Sandringham, and although he rather dreaded them, his broadcasts had proved immensely popular. On the evening of 6 May he broadcast to the empire with a heartfelt and rather humbling message:

> At the close of this memorable day, I must speak to my people everywhere. How can I express what is in my heart? ... I can only say to you, my very dear people, that the Queen and I thank you from the depths of our hearts for all the loyalty — and may I say so? — the love, with which this day and always you have surrounded us. I dedicate myself anew to your service for all the years that may still be given me.

No one pretended that George V's reign had been a period of unalloyed happiness. On the contrary, every commentator remarked upon what truly dreadful events had occurred during his rule, with the Great War being the worst. In his address at the service of thanksgiving, the Archbishop of Canterbury remarked that the king's reign contained many 'years of almost unbroken anxiety and strain'. But the king's conduct, dignity and leadership during a period of unparalleled difficulty had earned him the respect and affection of his subjects.

Cheap and colourful, tin stick-pin badges like this were immensely popular and were often given away by manufacturers of household goods.

Enamel and metal badges have proved to be lasting mementoes of the 1935 jubilee. Both of these show simple profiles of the king and queen, with enamelling in patriotic red, white and blue.

THE JUBILEES OF
ELIZABETH II

ELIZABETH II may or may not become Britain's longest-lived queen, but she has certainly enjoyed more jubilee celebrations than any other British monarch. Aged only twenty-five when she came to the throne in 1952, she has been blessed with good health and a long life, two factors vital to the celebration of multiple jubilees.

It is a truism to say that the world has changed during the sixty years of Elizabeth II's rule, but arguably attitudes to royalty have altered far more since 1952 than they did, say, during Queen Victoria's reign. Respect and deference are less widespread; the question of whether Britain wants or can afford a monarchy, or even whether it is right to have one, is frequently discussed. The queen has been widely praised for her enduring dignity and ability to maintain the status of the British crown, which as an office is greater than the power of one single individual; herein lies the root of her success as a monarch.

THE SILVER JUBILEE, 1977

The festivities of the Queen's Silver Jubilee in 1977 owed much to the precedent set in 1935, but with the nation emerging from the energy crisis under the control of a tired Labour government and the glint of safety pins in the noses and clothes of the nation's anarchic punk youth, it seemed unlikely that the great British public would be persuaded to celebrate the jubilee of a queen who represented what many regarded as an outdated institution. Pessimists in government were reluctant to commit funds to extravagant celebrations, and bureaucrats were urged to encourage local festivities such as street parties. The Permanent Under Secretary at the Home Office, Sir Arthur Peterson, stressed that there were two principles to bear in mind when planning an event:

> You must not bore the Public.
> You must not kill the Queen.

Judged by these austere criteria, the 1977 jubilee was a roaring success.

Opposite:
Street parties like this one in Beverley Road, east London, were held all over the country for the first time since the coronation in 1953. It was a novelty for the younger generation and a chance to recapture community spirit.

The Silver Jubilee of 1977 stands out because for the first time the monarch celebrated by travelling abroad to visit her people. In 1887, 1897 and 1935, representatives of the dominions and colonies had come to London to pay their respects to their imperial sovereign. A very clear objective of the 1977 jubilee was that the Queen should visit every country in the Commonwealth over which she reigned, as well as touring the British Isles.

Above: This statue of Elizabeth II in Regina, Saskatchewan, was commissioned to celebrate her Golden Jubilee in 2002. It shows the Queen on Burmese, her favourite horse, which was presented to her in 1969 by the Royal Canadian Mounted Police.

Right: During the Silver Jubilee year of 1977 the Queen and the Duke of Edinburgh travelled to as many parts of the United Kingdom as they could. On 20 June 1977, the Queen visited Preston in Lancashire.

The Queen and the Duke of Edinburgh visited Butterley, near Ripley, Derbyshire, to open the Derbyshire Police Headquarters.

Members of the royal family wave to crowds from Buckingham Palace balcony after the thanksgiving service on 7 June 1977. From left to right: Princess Anne, Earl Mountbatten of Burma, Captain Mark Phillips, the Queen, the Duke of Edinburgh.

The official souvenir crown coin (with a face value of twenty-five pence) issued for the 1977 jubilee incorporated an equestrian portrait of the Queen on the obverse. The reverse depicted the ampulla and anointing spoon used in the coronation ceremony.

It was an ambitious aim, and initially the government was opposed to the idea because of the cost, but the foreign tours were a huge success. In February the Queen and Prince Philip visited Australia, New Zealand and the western Pacific islands of Tonga, Western Samoa, Fiji, and Papua New Guinea. In October it was the turn of Canada and the Caribbean. The royal yacht *Britannia* ferried the Queen to many destinations, and as one courtier remembered, 'Everywhere we went, we had these aquatic welcomes: boats, people – harbour entrances would be just packed with people everywhere.'

In Britain, 'jubilee fever' was lukewarm in the early months of the year, but when the main events began in June, public interest gradually increased. The Queen walked up Snow Hill at the end of the Long Walk in Windsor Great Park on 6 June to light the first bonfire in a chain of beacons that would blaze across Britain. The next day crowds numbering nearly a million people watched the procession of the royal family from Buckingham Palace to St Paul's Cathedral for the official Service of Thanksgiving. The scenes in London recalled those of her coronation: many people had camped out in the Mall overnight and the royal coachmen recalled that the noise of cheering on the journey to St Paul's was just one 'almighty roar'. Once again, the Queen broke with tradition, and after the cathedral service she went

The Silver Jubilee Walkway was inaugurated by the Queen on 9 June 1977, and was intended to link some of London's most famous landmarks. The route was marked by circular plaques at every junction and by marker poles. Now known as the Jubilee Walkway, it was updated for the Golden Jubilee, and in 2012 will include the Jubilee Greenway, connecting the 2012 Olympic venues.

on a royal 'walkabout' through the City. It was all carefully planned amid tight security, but it demonstrated the changing face of the British monarchy: neither Queen Victoria nor King George V ever mingled so closely with so many of their subjects.

While the Queen lunched at the Guildhall with the Lord Mayor, the rest of the country proved that they had entered into the spirit of the jubilee and enjoyed street parties (there were four thousand in London alone), processions and fêtes. In that respect, community celebrations remained remarkably similar to those of the 1935 jubilee. As in 1935, when the nation was slumped in an economic depression, people used the jubilee as a chance to cheer themselves up with fancy-dress competitions, parties and sporting events. In 1977, it was the first time in a generation that the British had a good excuse for a national celebration, and many people remarked on how the street parties and games united communities and allowed them to get to know their neighbours.

On 9 June, and in emulation of her Elizabethan namesake, the Queen embarked on a river progress up the Thames. She held a lunch party aboard the royal yacht *Britannia* and opened the Silver Jubilee Walkway and the South Bank Jubilee Gardens, before reviewing the river pageant from County Hall. The Silver Jubilee Walkway (now known simply as the Jubilee Walkway) was one of the most successful and lasting memorials from 1977. Intended to connect some of London's most famous

Jubilee souvenirs ranged from traditional ceramic mugs and coasters, via patriotic badges, to almost anything that could be decorated with a Union Jack. The Sex Pistols' single, 'God Save the Queen', was an anarchic re-working of the National Anthem, and was banned by the BBC.

Opposite:
The royal family processing down the aisle of St Paul's for the Service of Thanksgiving on 4 June 2002. The Queen and the Duke of Edinburgh are followed by the Prince of Wales and his sons, Prince William and Prince Harry, with Prince Andrew behind them.

The Queen and the Duke of Edinburgh in the Gold State Coach returning from St Paul's Cathedral in 2002.

landmarks, it was expanded at the time of the Golden Jubilee in 2002 and now traverses 15 miles of the city.

The 1977 Silver Jubilee was deemed a great success and many people still remember it fondly, although one sign of the times was the single, 'God Save the Queen' released by the anarchic punk band, the Sex Pistols. Nihilistic and considered to be in bad taste, it reached number two in the charts, despite being banned by Radio One.

However, most of the nation enjoyed the celebration, perhaps no one more than the Queen herself, who was touched and surprised by the reception she received throughout her realms. 'I am simply amazed, I had no idea', she said more than once.

THE GOLDEN JUBILEE, 2002

Twenty-five years later, public attitudes to royal celebrations had changed again. In the intervening years the Queen's children had married and divorced; the heir to the throne had confessed adultery on national television and the death of his ex-wife in a car crash had provoked an outpouring of national grief on a scale never previously witnessed. The British opinion of their royal family was one in which deference barely registered, but interestingly, the Queen herself was consistently singled out as worthy of their respect and affection. Public interest in the monarchy had, if anything,

increased since 1977, although that attention was often highly intrusive.

The year of the Golden Jubilee had an inauspicious beginning, with the deaths of the Queen's sister, Princess Margaret, and her 101-year-old mother. Despite these sad events, the jubilee plans went ahead unaltered. A Golden Jubilee weekend of events was scheduled for 1–4 June 2002.

The Party at the Palace was unlike any other jubilee celebration before it, with rock guitarist Brian May playing 'God Save the Queen' on the roof of Buckingham Palace. It was the first time that the gardens of Buckingham Palace had been used for a public concert.

Mindful of the enormity of the event, the plans were announced in Parliament by the Prime Minister, Tony Blair:

The Queen has said that she sees her Golden Jubilee as an opportunity to express her thanks for the support and loyalty she has enjoyed during her reign. She hopes that events surrounding the Jubilee will create numerous opportunities for voluntary and community service and that as many people as possible will have the opportunity to enjoy the celebrations to mark this happy occasion.

Buckingham Palace was lit up with the most dramatic illuminations in its two-hundred-year history, to the delight of the million-strong crowd in the Mall.

The official Golden Jubilee logo adorns the reverse of this 2002 commemorative coin.

Thousands of school children received mugs, which were ordered by local authorities and schools to celebrate the event.

The government tried to ensure that as many people as possible could celebrate the event by offering the inducement of lottery funding to voluntary organisations and local groups who wished to provide some sort of lasting legacy. Individuals and corporate donors wishing to commemorate the jubilee with a financial donation were directed to five charities of which the Queen was patron.

The Queen circumnavigated the globe for the sixth time in her reign during her golden jubilee year, with visits to Jamaica, New Zealand, Australia and Canada. The Queen and Prince Philip also visited seventy cities and towns in fifty counties throughout the British Isles, and, in an echo of her grandfather's peregrinations throughout London in 1935, made separate visits to north, south, east and west London during May and June 2002. On 2 June, while the Queen and the Duke of Edinburgh worshipped in St George's Chapel, Windsor, her children attended services of thanksgiving around the country: the Prince of Wales in Swansea; the Princess Royal in Ayr; and the Earl of Wessex in Salisbury. All of the royal family took part in the official Service of Thanksgiving at St Paul's Cathedral on 4 June. The Queen lit the jubilee beacon, which was mounted on the Victoria Memorial outside Buckingham Palace, on 3 June. It was the first in a chain of 2,002 beacons, which stretched beyond the British Isles, from the Arctic to the Antarctic, embracing Commonwealth countries across the globe.

The events of the Golden Jubilee were purposely designed to be inclusive and accessible to all the Queen's subjects. The Queen visited all the main faith communities – Christian, Jewish, Muslim, Hindu and Sikh – in Britain during her jubilee year and hosted a multi-faith reception at Buckingham Palace for over seven hundred representatives of different faiths. Across the Atlantic, in New York, the Empire State Building shone purple and gold on the evening of 4 June 2002, in honour of the close ties between Britain and the United States. There were some imaginative new additions to the traditional celebrations. People born on 6 February 1952, the Queen's accession day, were invited to garden parties in London and Edinburgh, part of a series of six jubilee garden parties, attended by a total of 48,000 guests. During the Golden Jubilee weekend, a rock concert was held in the gardens of Buckingham Palace, which came to be known as the 'Party at the Palace'. The headline act was Brian May, the lead guitarist of the rock group Queen, who launched into a rendition of 'God Save the Queen' from the chimney pots of the palace roof. Some twelve thousand people watched from the palace gardens, having won their tickets in a lottery, while a million more enjoyed the spectacle on big screens in the Mall. It also attracted a huge worldwide television audience of some two hundred million viewers.

The official emblem for Queen Elizabeth's Diamond Jubilee was designed by ten-year-old Katherine Dewar, whose design was chosen from over thirty-five thousand entries in a Blue Peter competition.

THE DIAMOND JUBILEE, 2012

The Queen has not only survived long enough to celebrate her Golden Jubilee in 2002 and her Diamond Jubilee in 2012, but the public, far from being bored by royal celebrations (as feared in 1977) has entered into the spirit of patriotic display. There is undoubtedly an element of wry irony among some quarters of the population who regard excessive displays of flag-waving patriotism as rather vulgar, but the wedding of Prince William in 2011 showed that almost everyone enjoys a free public holiday and many people are prepared to deck their homes in bunting and flags.

More than one thousand boats are expected to take part in the Thames River Pageant on 3 June 2012. It will be led by the Queen, who will be aboard the royal barge, and is expected to raise some £100 million for charitable causes. (William Dudley, © Royal Household)

With a service of thanksgiving in St Paul's and a grand river pageant planned on the Thames, observers could be forgiven for thinking that jubilee celebrations have barely altered in the past 150 years. But the changes are subtle and reflect the spirit of the age. In keeping with the ecological concerns of the twenty-first century, the Diamond Jubilee will be marked by the planting of six million trees across the UK. Buckingham Palace will launch the Big Jubilee Lunch on 3 June, a 2012 spin on the traditional jubilee street party, which is an initiative to encourage community involvement.

Where will it all end? Elizabeth II's seventieth anniversary is not an impossibility and would be quite remarkable by any standards. Although she would by then be Britain's longest-reigning monarch, she would be outdone on the international stage by others. Louis XIV of France managed seventy-two years, and the current record-holder of the longest monarchical reign is the late King Sobhuza II of Swaziland, who succeeded to the throne as a small infant and reigned for eighty-two years, from 1899 until 1982. The Queen's immediate successors are certainly unlikely to enjoy such long reigns.

Britain is no longer the most powerful nation on earth and so the nation's jubilee celebrations have altered from jingoistic displays to ceremonial pageants overlaid with a strong feeling of philanthropy. The occasion is now regarded as an opportunity to do good and the nineteenth-century letter-writers who pleaded with the authorities to spend money on poor-relief rather than frivolous illuminations would no doubt be impressed with the charitable aims of the jubilees of the twenty-first century.

After a lifetime of service to the nation, the Queen and the Duke of Edinburgh show very little sign of easing up in their schedule of official events.

FURTHER READING

Some of these titles are out of print, but are reasonably easy to obtain via second-hand book sites on the Internet.

Coley, Linda. *Britons – Forging the Nation 1707–1837.* Yale University Press, 1992.

Hibbert, Christopher. *George III: A Personal History.* Viking, 1998.

Hibbert, Christopher (ed.). *Queen Victoria in her Letters and Journals.* Penguin, 1985.

Lacey, Robert. *Monarch.* The Free Press, 2002.

Longford, Elizabeth. *Victoria R.I.* Weidenfeld & Nicolson, 1964.

Pimlott, Ben. *The Queen.* HarperCollins, 1996.

Pope-Hennessy, James. *Queen Mary.* Allen and Unwin, 1959.

Rose, Kenneth. *George V.* Weidenfeld & Nicolson, 1983.

Shawcross, William. *Queen and Country.* BBC, 2002.

Wilson, A.N. *The Victorians.* Hutchinson, 2002.

PLACES TO VISIT

Monuments to the jubilees of Queen Victoria, George V and Elizabeth II are scattered throughout Britain and the world, particularly in countries that were once part of the British Empire or remain in the Commonwealth.

LONDON
Buckingham Palace, London SW1A 1AA
Telephone: 020 7766 7300
Website: www.royalcollection.org.uk

The Jubilee Walkway
Website: www.jubileewalkway.org

St Paul's Cathedral, St Paul's Churchyard, London EC4M 8AD.
Telephone: 020 7246 8350
Website: www.stpauls.co.uk

Westminster Abbey, 20 Dean's Yard, London SW1P 3PA
Telephone: 020 7222 5152
Website: www.westminster-abbey.org

Windsor Castle, Windsor SL4 1NJ
Telephone: 020 7930 9625
Website: www.royalcollection.org.uk

ELSEWHERE IN BRITAIN

Birmingham: Monument to Lord Nelson unveiled on Jubilee Day, 1809, Bullring.

Chester: Eastgate Clock, Eastgate St, Chester.

Lincoln: Bust of George III (once on Dunston Pillar), Castle Hill, Lincoln LN1 3AA.

Skegness: 1897 Jubilee Clock Tower, Lumley Road, Skegness, Lincolnshire PE25 3NA.

Weymouth: King's Statue (George III), The Esplanade, Weymouth, Dorset DT4 7AN; 1887 Jubilee Clock, A353, Weymouth, Dorset DT4 8DN.

Windsor: Golden Jubilee Statue of Elizabeth II, Queen Anne's Ride, Great Park; Obelisk commemorating the 1809 National Jubilee celebrations, Bachelors Acre.

CANADA

Perth County Court House, Stratford, Ontario (built 1887).

Regina Saskatchewan: Golden Jubilee statue of Elizabeth II.

Jubilee statues of Queen Victoria abound all over the world, notably in Abingdon, Oxfordshire (1887); College Green, Bristol (1887); Southend-on-Sea, Essex (1897); Windsor, Berkshire (1887); Doulton Fountain, Glasgow (1887); the Great Hall, Winchester Castle, Hampshire (1887); Pietermaritzburg, South Africa (1887); Victoria Memorial Hall, Kolkata, India (1897); Manitoba Diamond Jubilee Monument, Winnipeg, Canada (1897); Parliament Hill, Ottawa, Canada (1897).

INDEX